HEART IGNITE

166 Engaging Prayer Experiences for All Ages

THE
Youth & Family
INSTITUTE

HEART IGNITE

Published by:
The Youth & Family Institute
www.tyfi.org

Written by:
Diane Monroe
Associate Director for Youth Education and Confirmation
Division for Congregational Ministries, ELCA, Chicago, Illinois
www.elca.org/eteam

and

Lyle Griner
National Director for Peer Ministry
The Youth & Family Institute, Bloomington, Minnesota
www.peerministry.org

Editing and layout by:
Carolyn Berge

Cover photograph:
budgetstockphoto.com

ISBN 1-889407-45-3

TABLE OF CONTENTS

....

WHAT THIS IS
....

This is a compilation of creative ways to enter into prayer. Some you have experienced before, others will be new. Some you will use, some you won't, and some you will change or even combine to fit your own situation and style. These collections are edited together from two separate lists of prayers collected over the years by Diane and Lyle. Many of them come from our own experiences in small groups, camps, families, educational experiences and worship. Others have contributed by sharing their ideas with us. Some come from our own imaginations. We have tried hard to not use printed ideas that are unique to a particular resource.

Who will find these ideas helpful?

- Families for candle and devotion times
- Confirmation leaders
- Creative worship leaders
- Youth group leaders
- Small group leaders
- Camp counselors
- Sunday school teachers
- Retreat leaders
- Church schoolteachers
- Peer Ministry facilitators
- Pastors
- And you!

FOREWORD

Today I wrote a letter, conversed on the phone, e-mailed a friend, looked up some Web pages, read some out of a book, waved at a friend, drew a diagram, honked at a car that almost ran me off the road, talked one-on-one to a friend, thought of a new idea, hugged a friend, kissed my wife, gave a report at a meeting, laughed at a joke, sang a song in the shower, sang another one with the radio, and hung a sign outside my door that said "don't interrupt." Communication is constant. It happens in many different forms. It reveals my emotions, divulges my thoughts, clarifies my opinions, relays facts, announces my beliefs, recounts my day, and hints at my personality. So how many ways and topics may there be to communicate to God? We are convinced that everything can lead to prayer. Read these ideas and you will see what we mean.

LIGHTING A CANDLE

There has always seemed to be something magical about lighting a candle. I learned early on as a youth minister that I could talk about anything, even with a group of junior high guys, in a dark room, lying on our bellies, with a candle burning in the center. I have also learned that families thirst for time when they can discover the spiritual light in their midst. Many of the prayers in this collection may guide your candletime prayers. Shut off the phone, the TV, and lights. Do whatever you need to help your group, your family, or yourself ignite your hearts in prayer and conversation.

ACTS PRAYER ◄·······

There are many ways to use this model. One is to pair up with another person to share specifically about each area. After coming back together ask participants to pray one-word prayers based on their conversations.

A—ADORATION or ACCLAMATION, praise for who God is

C—CONFESSION, confessing of sins and weaknesses

T—THANKSGIVING, thanking God for blessings

S—SUPPLICATION, our deepest needs for ourselves and others

The children and youth who work with Lauren, a youth and family ministry friend, remember this simple format by making necklaces, bracelets, or anklets using beads with letters imprinted on them.

1

PLEASE, SORRY, THANK YOU

These three little words will help our wee brothers and sisters with their first prayers. Don't assume though, that this simple prayer reminder is only for small children. This simple pattern readily provides a memory tool for all who come before God in prayer.

TRIP PRAYER ←········┐

Here's an acronym prayer *a la* Martin Luther, who invites us
to take a prayer TRIP by suggesting we offer prayers of:

T—THANKSGIVING

R—REGRET (confession of sins and weakness)

I—INTERCESSION (prayers on behalf of others)

P—PURPOSE (what God wants from us)

3

SEED PRAYER

This is a great way to conclude an event and to help partici-pants carry into their daily lives what they experienced together. Give each person a packet of five seeds. As each petition is prayed ask participants to hold up one of the seeds. Responses to each petition can either be spoken or held in silent, individual reflection.

God of the soil, speak in the hearts of those present today that your message of love and grace is firmly planted to nurture and support.... (Pray a summary of the experience.)

God of the seeds, inspire our words, our thoughts, our hearts to grow into.... (Pray for ongoing growth.)

4

God of the sower, strengthen us with your spirit in the easy times and the difficult times that we.... (Pray about the needs and concerns of the participants.)

God of the sun and the rain, pour down upon us all that we need to be Christ-like in order to.... (Pray about the mission and purpose of the participants.)

Be in us, be with us, be above us, be beside us.... (Pray for each member by name.) *Amen*

FLASH PAPER PRAYER

Flash paper is a type of paper that can be purchased at most magic supply stores. As soon as the paper touches a flame it disappears—in a flash. Not even ashes remain. Give each participant a piece of flash paper to write a prayer of confession. Begin with silent prayers of confession and then invite each person to hold his or her paper over a lit candle. Offer the reminder that God's grace and forgiveness is always available for each person and is final and complete.

5

DICE PRAYER

No, this is isn't prayer *a la* Vegas! This really is a great tool for learning the various elements of prayer. Create a die using a wooden block. Draw or paste pictures of various symbols on each side. Each person takes a turn rolling the die, then says a prayer that fits the symbol rolled. Make several different dice. Some examples to get you rolling:

- Gingerbread person—gifts you're glad God has given you

- Compass—direction and guidance

- Sad face—forgiveness

- Broken heart—prayers for someone who is hurting

- Globe—world concerns and leaders

- Cross—praise and honor recognizing God

- Footprints—people and places God put in your path today

6

HEART IGNITE: ENGAGING PRAYER EXPERIENCES

KOOSH® BALL PRAYER

This one may have roots in Native American culture. The only person talking is the person holding the "coo-stick." Holding a physical item seems to give a person the needed encouragement or moment of opportunity to speak, or, in this case, to pray.

One person begins by holding the Koosh® ball (or other appropriate object such as a different type of ball, a pine cone, cross, or balloon), offering a prayer, and then passing the object to someone else. Continue until all have held the object and offered a prayer.

PAINT CHIP PRAYER ←┄┄┄┄┄

Collect multiple paper strips with color samples from a
paint store. Cut off the names of the colors so that people
react to their immediate emotions stirred by the color
instead of the label. Ask each person to pick a color that
represents a scenario to pray for. Any scenario will work,
but here are a few examples:

• A current need

• A cause for celebration

• A hope or dream

• A fear or worry

• A memory

As each person shares an explanation through prayer,
conclude with "Lord in your mercy...hear our prayer."

HEART IGNITE: ENGAGING PRAYER EXPERIENCES

FILE-IT-AWAY PRAYER

This prayer format is wonderful for children and families. You'll need manila file folders for each person, self-stick note paper, colorful stickers, and markers to decorate. With markers and stickers decorate the outside (and some on the inside) of a folder. Then write a prayer concern and several self-stick notes and place them inside on the right-hand side of the folder. Pray about them daily. At the end of a week's time, consider each prayer concern. If the prayer has been answered, move that note to the left side of the folder. If the concern is cause for continual prayer, keep the note on the right-hand side.

9

TELEPHONE PRAYER ◄┈┈┈┈┐

Praying in a conversational manor may be best compared to having a conversation with a good friend on the telephone. The friends share their day's events, their relationships, their fears, and even the things they did wrong. Pass an unplugged telephone around, encouraging participants to talk to God as if they were talking to a good friend.

10

CHAIR PRAYER

Place a chair in the middle of the room. Read Matthew 18:20: "For where two or three are gathered in my name, I am there among them." Let the chair represent Christ's presence. Pray-ers direct their eyes toward the open chair and verbally pray from the heart.

Thad, a youth minister in Texas, was amazed at the powerful sense of Christ's presence that came over him during this prayer.

11

PUZZLE PRAYER ←┄┄┄┄┄┄┄┄┐

Use a simple children's puzzle with large pieces. (Diane gave up her favorite Porky Pig puzzle to create this one!) Either spray paint over the picture to create a blank writing surface, or use the back of the puzzle pieces. On each puzzle piece, print some of the following words and phrases: *thanksgiving, adoration, concern for a friend, world issue, leader of our country, a family member,* and other appropriate prayer suggestions.

Distribute puzzles pieces equally among the participants. Build the puzzle a piece at a time, inviting each person to share a short prayer according to the topic. The completed puzzle is a visual reminder of how we support one another in the midst of life's joys and struggles.

12

PICTURES-OF-JESUS PRAYER

Collect various icons, paintings, or pictures of Jesus. Lay them out for everyone to view. Invite each person to pick one and to offer a prayer of praise and honor reflecting some of the attributes they may see in the artist's works.

13

BUILDING BLOCK PRAYER ←·······

Set a pile of blocks off to the side. Place one block on the table proclaiming Christ as the cornerstone of faith. Invite each participant to add a block in a creative way to the cornerstone, while offering a prayer petition. The finished creation may look like a building, tower, path, or some other structure. Let everyone share thoughts or meaning seen in the creation.

14

POCKETFUL OF PRAYER

15

Shelly flips through her keys. "My keys remind me of my whole life. One is about home and family, another work. Here's the key to Dad's storage unit at the nursing home. This extra key is for my son's car at college." Her key ring represents the very people Shelly prays for daily.

Our best prayer reminders may be in our pockets. Invite each person to choose one item from their pocket or purse as a symbol for ongoing prayers. Share stories and prayers.

SHOW-AND-TELL PRAYER ◄·············┐

Here is one that might remind many of us of our first school years. Remember Show and Tell? "My dog, Cinder, died this week," or "This is the present my Grandma sent me from Alaska." Bring objects or stories to share for your prayer time. Use the stories that are told as opportunities to pause for prayer for each situation and the special people involved.

16

PRAYER DOTS

Prince of Peace Lutheran Church, Burnsville, Minnesota, has been seeing spots for years! Every Sunday, worshipers are invited to place a green dot sticker on their watches or cell phones as a constant reminder that all times are good times to pray. Select stickers that represent a particular theme or a season.

17

PRAYER CONNECTION TIME ←·············

Build your community or enhance your family life by asking everyone to pause at a pre-determined time each day, for a moment of prayer on behalf of each other. Give each person a tiny sticker to place on his or her watch as a reminder.

18

INVISIBLE INK PRAYER

Use a toothpick, an old ink pen, or a cotton swab dipped in lemon or onion juice to write a prayer. Let it dry thoroughly. To reveal the prayer, hold the paper over a candle, light bulb, or hot iron. As the paper warms—*voila!*—the words will appear.

19

LIGHT SHOW PRAYER ◄·······················

Turn the lights off and soft music on. Give each person a
flashlight (colored tissue paper over the light adds variety).
With each petition offered, turn the flashlights on and off.
This can be done in circle fashion or randomly, creating an
interesting light show. Close with, "Jesus is the light of the
world. Amen."

20

SPOTLIGHT AFFIRMATION PRAYER

Hang a single light in a dark room. One at a time, have participants sit in the middle of the circle underneath the light. Remaining participants offer prayers of thanks for the spotlighted person's specific gifts, personality traits, talents, and contributions to the group.

21

SONG PRAYER ◄┄┄┄┄┄┄┄┐

Music is an expression of the soul. We find powerful prayers in hymns, camp songs, praise, and worship songs.

Sing *a cappella* or with musical instruments or recordings; with eyes closed or open; holding hands or raising arms toward the sky; or in motion and movement. Recognize the words and melodies as a unifying prayer tradition.

22

BOOM BOX PRAYER

Recorded songs from Christian and secular sources hold great meditative potential. One youth and family minister asks youth to choose a CD and then plays a song from it at the end of their small-group time. As others meditate on the song, the youth share personal reflections of how the words and music speak of life and faith. It is amazing how often youth hear God's voice in songs—even more often than the writer most likely intended. While many adults listen for objective meanings, many youth seem to hear with subjective ears.

23

MUSICAL MEDITATION PRAYER

Several months after a service project, one youth group created a makeshift sacred space with a hammer, a picture of a family whose house they worked on, a pair of gloves, and a cross. They played "My Hands Are Small" by singer-songwriter Jewel. It was a holy moment.

Pick a song that provokes thoughts, memories, hopes, or other such reflections for your group. Set the mood with dimmed lights. Create a focal point of symbols that reflect themes of the song. Play the song, inviting people to silently meditate, listen for God's voice, and silently share prayers.

24

FAMILIAR SOUNDS PRAYER

25

Our senses trigger thoughts and memories. Record a collection of various audio sounds. Play one sound at a time, inviting participants to share thoughts and prayers (verbally or silently) generated by the sounds. Consider sounds such as a infant's cry, an ambulance siren, a bird singing, laughter, the ocean, or a short excerpt from Martin Luther Kings Jr.'s "I Have a Dream" speech. Almost any sound could be used. (Well, maybe not every sound!)

HYMN BOOK PRAYER ◄┄┄┄┄┄┄┄┐

Give each participant a book of familiar hymns. Invite each
to select a hymn and to tell of its significance. It may be a
hymn that was sung at a grandparent's funeral, or one that
she or he has heard since early childhood. Read some of
your favorite lines or a verse as a prayer.

26

NEWSPAPER PRAYER

One evening when they noticed the day's newspaper was just lying on the floor, several family members grabbed a section and randomly began sharing headlines or quick synopses of local and global happenings. The newspaper was transformed into a source for prayer. In liturgical tradition the person said, "Lord, in your mercy," and automatically the group responded, "Hear our prayer." As the sharing of stories continued, so did the responses. This has become a favorite family candletime.

27

MAP A PRAYER ◄·············

Post a map (world, country, or community) in a prominent place at home or at church. From time to time, gather around the map and give everyone small stickers or pushpins to indicate where there are concerns for prayer. Floods in India may prompt a dot on your world map. On a local map, mark the address of a friend whose father just lost his job. Conclude with spoken prayers.

28

LIGHT-OF-THE-WORLD PRAYER

29

Occasionally, Jeremy takes the map off the wall and places it on a table. Each person is given tea-lights to indicate where prayers are needed. This is a great way to infuse prayers with the reminder that Christ is the light of the world.

"WHERE IN THE WORLD?" PRAYER

Vary the previous idea (Light-of-the-World Prayer) by laying a world map on the floor and giving each person a penny. Each person chooses a country by closing eyes and tossing a penny onto the map. The group can help each other describe what they know about people in this area of the world, lifting up issues and people in prayer.

30

HEADLINE NEWS PRAYER

Gather around the television at news time. As each story is reported, have someone say, "Lord in your mercy." Others respond with, "Hear our prayers." Use a previously taped broadcast to better suit your schedule. Taping also is advantageous when you want to hit the pause button between stories in order to pray in greater detail.

31

AROUND-THE-WORLD PRAYER

Place a globe in the center of the table. Spin the globe as participants close their eyes while lightly touching the globe with one finger. Where the finger lands on the globe becomes the focus of prayer for each person. Brainstorm any information the group may have regarding living conditions, customs, or current affairs of the people in that area. Offer a prayer for our brothers and sisters in that county, their quality of life, and for their political leaders.

32

BRACELET PRAYER

This prayer is especially appropriate during Lent. Create a bracelet using string or leather strips and colored beads, one of each color listed below. Lead participants in prayer as the beads are distributed and placed on the strings.

33

- Black—for the suffering and death Jesus endured for my sin

- Red—for Christ's love for me, represented in the sacrificial blood

- White—for the joy of the Easter resurrection

- Blue—for the waters of baptism that set me free

- Green—for new life in Christ

- Yellow—for Jesus, the light of the world

- Clear—that through me, others see Christ

HEART IGNITE: ENGAGING PRAYER EXPERIENCES

COUNTING BEADS PRAYER ◀┄┄┄┄┄┄┐

Bead and *pray* share word origins. Roman Catholic brothers and sisters pray with the rosary, a designated number of beads and spaces with specific religious significance.

String beautiful glass beads on a ribbon. What number would you use? Maybe one for each member in your family; 12 for the disciples; 150 for each of the psalms; or six for each of the days you are at camp.

34

EGG CARTON PRAYER

Write a daily prayer on a slip of paper and place it in one of the sections of an empty egg carton. The prayers may be of praise, thanksgiving, concern, or anything else you desire to take to the Lord.

Remember Psalm 91:4: "He will cover you with his feathers, and under his wings you will find refuge" (NIV). Since it takes 21 days for eggs to hatch, give these "pray eggs" to the Lord. At the end of three weeks, reread your prayers and discover ways that God has answered.

35

PAPER CHAIN PRAYER

Cut a series of paper strips of various colors to have available at prayer times. Invite participants to write prayer petitions on strips of paper, then link them together in a chain. This can be done over a series of gatherings to create an ever-growing chain. You may want to hang the chain around a room, creating a space that is encircled by prayer.

36

LITURGICAL SEASON PRAYER

On squares of cardstock, draw or glue symbols to represent the church season or a congregational emphasis. Link the squares with colored string and tape and hang them as prayer reminders. For example, make sandal cutouts to symbolize discipleship activities, or decorate an Epiphany tree or a Lenten tree with symbols of the season.

37

SCULPTURE PRAYER

Art can be a form of prayer. Creativity can be an expression of beliefs, feelings, thanksgiving, confession, and adoration. Invite your participants to create a prayer sculpture. Use clay, play dough, aluminum foil, or any other resources that are available. One brave leader even suggested shaving cream or mashed potatoes! Let people place their works of art at the altar, explaining their thoughts and their prayers.

38

ART

MOVEMENT PRAYER

Dance, drama, mime, clown routines, and other movement arts can be expressive interpretations of prayers. Such prayers can be presented by a performing group at camps, in worship, or for any other gathering. One example is to ask everyone to participate by forming bodies in a way that shows praise, sorrow for sins, hope about a concern for a friend, and so forth.

39

REFRIGERATOR ART PRAYER ◀·······

A child draws a picture, and presents it to a parent who admires it and gives a big hug. The picture is proudly displayed on the refrigerator. This prayer invites participants to draw a picture, images, or symbols that express their relationship with God. Imagine God looking at each gift with love and pride as the drawings are all hung on a refrigerator.

40

LORD'S PRAYER WITH RIBBONS

41

This is a tangible way to focus on the meaning of the Lord's Prayer. For each person, you'll need a 6" strip of ribbon of each of the colors listed below. Someone leads by speaking the first phrase (the first phrase of the Lord's Prayer) as everyone picks up the blue ribbon. The next petition is read while the white ribbons are tied to the end of the blue ribbons, and so on. Use the following order. When completed, speak the entire prayer together and explain what each color symbolizes.

• Blue (loving parent)—*Our Father who art in heaven...*

• White (holiness)—*Hallowed be thy name...*

• Purple (majestic)—*Thy kingdom come, thy will be done...*

- Green (earth)—*On earth as it is in heaven...*

- Yellow (wheat)—*Give us this day, our daily bread...*

- Red (Jesus' blood)—*Forgive us our trespasses, as we forgive those who trespass against us...*

- Orange (evil)—*Lead us not into temptation but deliver us from evil...*

- Gold (God's kingdom)—*For thine is the kingdom, the power and the glory, forever and ever. Amen*

TOTEM POLE PRAYER

Larger sticks may be personalized by carving, drawing, or burning designs, thoughts, or scripture into the wood. Create a pole that celebrates the faith milestones, the memories of the week, the year or lifetime. Place the pole where it will be a reminder and celebration of God's working.

42

GODSPEED PRAYER ←

Someone is leaving for vacation. A youth has to leave the retreat early. A family member is going on a business trip, off to camp, or staying at Grandma's overnight. Surround this person with God's travel mercies by asking others to lay a hand on his or her head or shoulders. Share prayers for safe journey, for being Christ's light and for a safe return.

43

PRAYER JOURNEY

Create an imaginative journey through a series of prayer stations. The stations may center around themes such as the liturgical year, social-justice issues, or various generations. Post written directions at each station.

44

- Create a passport-like booklet/map to serve as a guide for each prayer experience.

- Leave mementos at each station for participants to take with them for ongoing prayers.

- Place tealight candles at one of the stations and invite participants to light one as they pray.

- Pick up a different color bead at each station to make into a bracelet.

- Have participants leave something, such as a prayer stone or artwork, at each station.

HEART IGNITE: ENGAGING PRAYER EXPERIENCES

PARALLEL PRAYER ◄┈┈┈┈┈┐

The youth thought it was awesome that as they pulled out of the church parking lot headed for the retreat center, their families and a few others from the church community gathered in the sanctuary along with the church leaders for prayers of safety for the journey and to invite God's spirit to be present at the retreat. In turn, the youth agreed to gather in the youth room just before the next church leaders' meeting was to begin to seek God's guidance and wisdom upon the issues at hand.

45

BIRTHDAY CANDLE PRAYER

Whether the occasion is a birthday, anniversary, or any other cause of celebration where cake and candles are present, it's an opportunity for prayers of affirmation and thanksgiving. Put the appropriate number of unlit candles in a pile beside the cake. Each person offers a prayer of thanks for a trait, a gift, or an act of kindness or friendship. As the prayer is said the candle is placed on the cake. Short, quick prayers, please—those candles burn fast!

46

WALKING PRAYER ←·····················

Walk together around a church building, camp property, or through the community. Pray for a specific ministry, for healing, for new life, for those living in the houses or apartments, for the shopkeepers, for thanksgiving or other special needs. Carry a cross, a candle, or some other symbol that holds meaning for your family or group.

47

BLESSING OF SACRED SPACE

Create a spiritual environment where your group or family will gather, anticipating the Holy Spirit's divine presence. Before others arrive, have one, two, or a group of people "walk the space"—touch objects or furniture, inviting God's Spirit to be present. Bless the nave, touching each pew before worshipers gather. Walk the Sunday school rooms or youth activity area. Bless your home before the small-group Bible study convenes.

48

JOGGING PRAYER ◄┈┈┈┈┈┈┐

Amber doesn't wear headphones when she is out for her morning run. Instead, she chooses this time to "be with God." Jogging, walking, swimming, or time on the treadmill is great for the body, and can also build a healthy spirit if we use the time to pray.

49

PARACHUTE PRAYER

Participants hold on to the perimeter of a parachute, large sheet, or piece of fabric. Each time a petition is offered, raise the sheet high, and then lower it slowly, feeling the air move from beneath. The motion of the sheet reminds us of the Holy Spirit's presence represented by wind and motion.

HUMAN SPOKES PRAYER ◄┈┈┈┈┈┈┐

This works well for a close-knit, fun-loving group. Invite everyone to lie on their backs with their heads all touching in the center, forming what may look like the spokes of a wheel. The experience is relaxing and creates an atmosphere conducive to prayer, especially if you are in an empty sanctuary with a cathedral style ceiling or looking up at a starlit sky.

51

JELLY ROLL PRAYER

Honor a person with prayer in this affectionate "bear hug."
The group stands in a straight line, holding hands, with the
person to be prayed for at the end. The end person begins to
lead the group in an inward spiral. Once the whole line has
spiraled around the honored person, tighten the spiral in a
giant hug and pray for the person in the center.

52

WEB PRAYER

One person begins by holding a ball of yarn or string and then offers a sentence prayer. He or she holds on to the end and tosses the ball to someone across the circle. This person offers a prayer, holds on to the string, and then tosses the ball to someone else. Continue until all are included in the web. Close by thanking God for the connected faith community.

At the end ask everyone to gently lay his or her connection on the ground. The string can be wound up without becoming a giant knot. To avoid tangles, make sure the ball is passed only on the upper side of the web.

53

SLAM DUNK PRAYER

It's amazing how ordinary actions become extraordinary occasions for prayer, praise, and thanksgiving. Kimberly noted how often kids in the youth group ran past the youth bulletin board and jumped up to give the top border a slam-dunk slap. Kim drew a large hand on colorful paper and tacked it high up on the bulletin board. Now those casual slam dunks are ritual moments for giving a high-five thanks to God.

54

BUBBLE GUM PRAYER ←··········

No doubt there's a pastor out there (most likely looking for a new call) that tried this one as part of a regular worship service! If you have a fun-loving, child-hearted group, allow each person to select a piece of bubble gum from a multi-colored package of gum balls. Colors often hold reminders of experiences or feelings. Ask each person to pray for something or someone brought to mind by the color of the bubble gum. Close with everyone blowing a big bubble for the "Amen."

55

FRUITS-OF-THE-SPIRIT PRAYER

Lay a variety of fresh fruit before participants. Invite each person to pick a type of fruit that in some way, shape, flavor, color, or possibly memory represents something about him- or herself. Have them share their thoughts. Read scripture— Galatians 5—on the fruits of the spirit. Let the group close by sharing thanksgiving prayers for the gifts and talents that make each person unique. Finish by letting people feast on the fruit.

56

M&M® PRAYER

Any candy that comes in a variety of colors will work.
(Using squares of colored paper is a low-calorie substitute.)
Beforehand, assign a designation for each color: green
may be for environmental issues around the world, red for
friends, blue for family, pink for the congregation, and so
on. After everyone selects a candy from the dish, read the
designations and give a few moments of reflection time.
Invite participants to use their color to pray about specific
issues or concerns.

57

CANDY HEART PRAYER

"Dear God, you rock my world!"

As Valentine's Day approaches, we begin to see those time-honored little candy hearts stamped with affectionate messages such as "You Rock," "Be Mine," and "Gotcha." Give every participant two or three candy hearts. Before they are tempted to snack, ask everyone to look at the messages they are holding in their hands. Invite each person to offer a brief prayer using the words or phrases found on their hearts.

58

PRETZEL PRAYER ←••••••••••

It is believed a monk first made pretzels in the fifth century in northern Italy. Monks spent a great deal of time in prayer with their arms folded over their chest as a sign of reverence. It seems an imaginative monk formed pieces of dough left over from bread baking into intriguing loops to mimic the shape. The baked shapes were given to children as a small reward for learning their prayers. He called it *pretiola*, which is Latin for "little reward."

Make your own homemade soft-dough pretzels. Talk about the origins of this tasty treat and how the pretzel is shaped to represent arms folded across the heart. Close with prayer and straight-from-the-oven treats! This makes a great wintertime family or group activity.

59

POPCORN PRAYER

Popcorn popping is a way to describe praying short, random petitions. Once somebody is ready to pray, they just pop in with praise, confession, thanksgiving, requests, or anything else. People may pop in several times as thoughts flow freely.

HEART IGNITE: ENGAGING PRAYER EXPERIENCES

MANGER PRAYER

The symbolism of preparing the manger for the coming of
Christ is a meaningful Advent activity. Set up an empty
manger with a small pile of hay next to it. Have participants
offer prayer petitions, and with the petition, place a piece
of hay in the manger. Leave the manger in an accessible
location where people can stop by for private prayers,
adding a piece of hay each time.

62

CHRISTMAS CARD PRAYER ◄┄┄┄┄┄┄┄┄┄

Celebrate the meaning of Christmas all year long by saving
Christmas cards. At least once a week take out one or more
cards. Read the cards and notes. Pray for the person who
sent the card, then respond with a letter, card, e-mail
message, or phone call telling the sender that he or she is
in your prayers.

63

GUIDED IMAGERY PRAYER

With eyes closed, in a relaxed position, take several deep breaths. Expand and enhance the following script to fit the situation and your group. Read slowly and pause frequently to allow the mind to paint a mental portrait.

Imagine you are walking on a road. Notice the location, the time of year, the sights, the sounds and aromas. What is on your mind as you walk?

After some time you notice a person walking ahead. Gradually, as you get closer, you sense that you know this person. The person turns and you recognize the man looking back at you. It is...Jesus! How do you greet? What are you compelled to say to Jesus? How does Jesus respond? How does that make you feel?

64

Jesus stops, looks in your eyes, and speaks to you.
What do you hear Jesus say?

Silently you walk together along the road. Notice the
sights, the sounds the aromas. What is on your mind as
you walk?

Ask participants, when they are ready and at their own pace,
to slowly open their eyes. Invite volunteers to share with
others their thoughts and emotions about the walk.

ANOINTING PRAYER

In James 5:14, prayers for healing follow anointing the sick with oil. Take turns praying for and anointing each other on the forehead with a drop of cooking oil or baby oil. The oil is a symbol of God's grace and acceptance. For centuries, anointing with oil has been a common practice to recognize or honor someone, and even was used when one was chosen to be a king. So it is that God accepts us and marks us as belonging to God.

65

SILENT MEDITATION PRAYER

Be still and know that I am God. —*Psalm 46:10*

Sit in silence, clearing all thoughts from the mind, and focus on a cross, a view of nature from a hill, or another object where God is recognized. Spend time just being in the presence of God.

BREATH-OF-THE-SPIRIT PRAYER

Center yourself for devotions or prayer with silence, allowing the Holy Spirit to shape your thoughts and words. As you inhale, think one phrase; use another phrase as you exhale.

Gracious God...give me peace.

Beautiful Savior...you are Lord of my life.

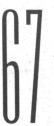

67

QUESTION PRAYER ←········

Many prayers include praise, requests, and confession, but
seldom do people bring their questions before God. Asking
questions may feel risky—like God is being doubted. But
"How do I know you exist?" is a very honest prayer. Asking,
"What is my calling and direction?" assumes one is intent on
listening for God. Invite participants to share their honest
questions to God.

68

QUAKER PRAYER

Do not worry about anything, but in everything by prayer and supplication with thanksgiving let your requests be made known to God. —Philippians 4:6

Find a place and a time where there will be no interruptions and conduct a prayer time in true Quaker tradition. Everyone enters the space in silence and sits and waits. As individuals are moved they may say verbal prayers, read a scripture passage, sing a song, share a thought, or express an emotion. When no one is speaking, silence and quiet mediation remain until the Holy Sprit again inspires another's spoken word. Create a non-anxious presence. The silence is as powerful as speech.

69

OPEN-ENDED PRAYER ◄┄┄┄┄┄┄┄┄┐

This is a prayer that is led, line by line, by a facilitator. The facilitator speaks the sentence fragment, inviting participants to randomly speak a word or short phrase to complete the sentence. Allow time for sufficient responses before moving on to the next sentence fragment. Examples may include:

70

- *God, you are _____.*

- *I thank you for _____.*

- *Forgive me for _____.*

- *I am concerned about _____.*

- *Give me strength to _____.*

- *Help me understand _____.*

- *As I talk with you I feel _____.*

GUIDED PRAYER

One at a time, pausing after each item, the leader suggests topics for the members to pray about silently. The leader might suggest praise, thankfulness, confession, healing, and so forth, or may say people's names in the group.

71

SERVICE AND PRAYER ◄········

Joni, a parent volunteer, wants her young people to be reminded of the central focus of service projects. Prior to each event she prepares index cards for each person identifying the task and a possible prayer mantra for the individual to repeat as they serve.

For example:

• Picking up trash—"Lifting Christ Higher"

• Serving meals at a shelter—"Use me, O Lord"

• Habitat for Humanity—"Be still and know that I am God"

72

PRAYER VIGIL

This ancient practice literally means "a watch kept during normal sleeping hours." Traditionally prayer vigils are kept through the night before Easter or during a time of emotional, spiritual, or physical trial. Consider including a vigil at the next youth lock-in for a concern of local or global nature. Invite participants to sign up for time slots.

73

"WHAT'S THAT I HEAR?" PRAYER

Begin in silence. Listen to the surrounding sounds. After a time of attentiveness and reflection, allow each person to offer a prayer guided by what they heard, felt, and sensed. Close with thanksgiving for the voices of those present.

74

CRESCENDO PRAYER

This is a favorite campfire prayer but can be effective in other situations also. Ask everyone to focus on a cross, a star in the sky, or another appropriate object. Repeat the Lord's Prayer first in a whisper, then building in volume until everyone is shouting the amen.

During one memorable campfire the group looked to the sky on one of those clear nights when every star ever created seems to be visible. As the group shouted the amen they were all treated to the gift of a spectacular shooting star.

75

LORD'S PRAYER MEDITATION

Ask everyone to sit in a comfortable position, relaxed and eyes closed. Begin by praying the Lord's Prayer together. The prayer is spoken again, but this time only by the facilitator who pauses after each petition for about one minute, allowing participants to pray silently their own words and heartfelt images.

76

WHISPER PRAYER

Dannica makes prayer friendly, especially for those intimidated by praying out loud. Each person cups their hands together and whispers a prayer into them. "Wait! Hold them there just a little longer!" As the prayer is concluded, Dannica counts 1-2-3 and the group throws their prayers into the air, releasing them to God's care with a triumphant "Amen."

77

BABBLING BROOK PRAYER ◄┄┄┄┄┄┄┐

A young youth minister moved from a position at a mainline denomination to a Pentecostal church. He recalls with a smile, "When I used to say 'Let's pray', it got real quiet. Now it gets real noisy!"

In some traditions everyone prays aloud at the same time. This profound experience holds particular meaning as we hear our own words spoken in the midst of a rushing steam of prayers.

78

MERGE PRAYER

This prayer might be compared to cars merging onto a busy highway. Everyone in the group prays silently. As each person concludes, at their own pace, they begin to repeat softly, "Thank you, God." By the end of the prayer, everyone has joined the flow of traffic in a common litany, saying in unison, "Thank you, God."

79

ANTIPHONAL PRAYER ←┄┄┄┄┄┄┄┐

After every petition prayed, this prayer concludes with a specific phrase. Others respond with another designated phrase. The psalms work well here.

Lord in your mercy….
Response: *Hear our prayer.*

For listening, God…
Response: *We praise your name.*

Give thanks to the Lord for he is good… (Psalm 106)
Response: *His steadfast love endures forever.* (Psalm 136)

80

DITTO PRAYER

If two of you agree on earth about anything you ask,
it will be done for you by my Father in heaven.
—Matthew 18:19

In some traditions it is common to verbally add one's agreement to another's spoken prayer. People sometime whisper "Yes, Lord" or "A-men." Even more expressive are the shouts of "Alleluia" or "Thank you, Jesus."

Encourage participants to come up with their own expressions to ditto their agreement for the petition. This may be a big traditional leap for some, but can also be a memorable shared experience.

81

PALMS PRAYER ◄┈┈┈┈┈┈┈┐

This prayer idea works best in pairs when prayers are to be said for each other. The person being prayed for extends his or her palms facing upwards. The person praying holds his or her hands above the other's, palms facing downward. The upward-facing palms symbolize our openness to receive the abundant blessings God has in store for us. The downward-facing palms are a reminder that God uses each one of us as a vessel to serve, support, and encourage one another through prayer.

82

CHAIN REACTION PRAYER

Start with everyone's hands at their side. As each person finishes praying she or he takes the hand of the person on the right. Continue letting each person pray until the circle is complete, the body of Christ, joined together as a family.

GIVING-AND-RECEIVING PRAYER

The group forms a circle with right palms turned upward, symbolizing the need to receive, and left palms turned downward, representing the act of giving and support. Then neighbors place their palms together, each downward-facing palm (left hands) on top of the upward-facing palms (right hands). Pray with hands connected in this fashion.

84

PEAKS-AND-VALLEY PRAYER

85

All in the group join hands with fingers intertwined. The leader explains the significance of this by holding up a hand with fingers spread apart. The tops of the fingers represent the high points in life, including strengths and gifts. The spaces between the fingers represents low points and weaknesses. With hands joined and fingers intertwined, neighbors' fingers fill in the valleys of each others' hands. God calls us to a full and rich faith lived out in community with others.

ELECTRICITY PRAYER

With eyes closed, hold hands in a circle. One person begins with a silent or spoken prayer and then squeezes the hand to the right. The prayer continues around the circle until the first person receives the "electric amen" back again.

86

HAND PRAYER

Hold your hand out in front of you, palm up, with fingers spread apart. Each digit represents a prompt for prayer:

• Thumb—closest to the heart, for family and friends

• First finger—the pointer finger, for those who nurture, guide, direct, or instruct us

• Second finger—the finger that stands tallest, for those who govern and have authority

• Third finger—the weakest finger, for those hurting, suffering, alienated, or treated unjustly

• Fourth finger—the smallest finger, a humble reminder to pray for oneself

• The whole hand—for God's loving palm, which supports us

SENSE-OF-TOUCH PRAYER

Blindfolded with soft music playing in the background, the group sits in a circle. One by one, objects are passed around for each person to touch, feel, hold, ponder, and meditate upon before sharing a brief prayer related to the object. A warm furry teddy bear might bring back childhood memories. A set of keys might conjure up the pleasant image of a first car for one person, while someone else recalls the pain of relinquishing offices keys after a recent lay-off. Other objects to pass: a large nail, a circle of thorns, a wood cross, a Bible, a loaf of bread, and a small globe of the world. The prayers will be varied and deeply moving.

Vary this idea with objects associated with a biblical story, seasons of the year, or other themes.

HIGH FIVE PRAYER

Your group doesn't like to hold hands? Or the group needs a new expression of prayer? Try a celebrative high five after each person prays. This is one where it might be best to keep eyes open lest someone gets bopped on the head by an overzealous pray-er!

89

ALTAR PRAYER ◄······

"We backpacked all week, each of us carrying our own small stone in our pocket. At first it seemed silly, but as the trip continued, the stone became my most important possession."

Each participant selects a stone with distinguishable characteristics of color or shape to become his or her prayer stone. As the group gathers for worship or devotions, pile all the stones together to create an altar where prayers are shared. Place a cross or candles on top. Afterward, have each person take his or her stone and carry it during the week. As the journey continues, the rock in each person's pocket is a tangible reminder of our relationship with God and others.

90

BRIGHT CAMPFIRE PRAYER

91

This prayer is also known as the Pyromaniac Prayer. Whatever you call it, it is a favorite and can be quite dramatic. You'll need a campfire or an indoor fireplace. Give each participant a supply of burnable twigs or sticks. The number and size of these sticks will depend on how big and how safe you want your fire to be! Invite individuals to lay a stick on the fire as they share their prayer petitions. Begin with a small fire and let it burn brighter and higher as each prayer is offered and a new stick added.

CAMPFIRE COALS PRAYER ◄┄┄┄┄┄┄┄┄┄┐

When sitting around the late-night campfire in the Boundary Waters Canoe Area of Minnesota, Dan, a guide, loved this demonstration. With a stick, roll burning coals away from the main fire, one for each participant in the group. Note that when each coal is not part of the main fire its brightness begins to fade. As the body of Christ, it is crucial that each individual stays connected to the main body or our light and witness also begins to fade. Pray for each participant by name, and as his or her name is spoken roll that coal back into the campfire. Watch as each coal once again burns brightly.

92

INCENSE PRAYER

Read Revelation 8:4: "And the smoke of the incense, with the prayers of the saints, rose before God from the hand of the angel." Incense has been used in worship for thousands of years. Light incense as you pray, heightening the experience with the unique element of mystical aromas.

93

TEALIGHT CANDLE PRAYER ←┄┄┄┄┄┄┄┄┄┐

"Tonight, instead of our usual prayer, let's each light a tealight candle for every new prayer topic," suggests Dad.

Kids and fire? Did this work? This family prayed for everything—including a drought in Africa, the neighbors' old dog, and a friend's aunt traveling somewhere in Germany. More than 50 candles lit the room before the final amen!

94

LIFE LIGHTING PRAYER

Set a candle on the floor in front of each person. The first person prays for another in the room and then lights the candle in front of that person. The person with the newly lit candle prays for someone else and lights that person's candle. This continues until everyone has been prayed for and all the candles are lit.

95

BLACK ROSE PRAYER

This prayer requires attention to your surroundings where you can't burn the wrong things, like furniture or forests! Prepare a cross, formed by two boards nailed together with a long nail, sharp end exposed, protruding out of the center. Give each person several squares of paper approximately 4" (1 dm) square. (At least 20 squares are needed for the desired effect.) Each person privately writes a prayer on each square. Attach the prayers to the cross by piercing the middle of the paper on the nail, in random fashion; you don't want the corners to line up. Light the edges of the paper with a match and observe silently. As the paper turns black, the edges curl forward, forming what looks like a black rose.

BURNING BARREL PRAYER

Instead of a full-blown campfire, Angela uses the bottom of a barrel outdoors for this prayer. She asks each person to write a sin or a struggle on a slip of paper and, with a silent prayer, to toss the paper into the barrel. When all the papers have been added to the barrel, Angela lights them on fire. Just as the flames consume the papers, so God reclaims our shortcomings and struggles.

97

CHRIST-AMONG-US PRAYER ←┄┄┄┄┄┄┄

Patsy's youth group begins every meeting by lighting a candle and inviting Christ's presence. During the lighting, the youth name people they want to lift up in prayer.

98

TODAY IS A GOOD DAY, TODAY IS A HARD DAY

Place a sheet of paper in the center of the group. Make two columns on the page. Title one column "Today Is a Good Day" and the other column "Today Is a Hard Day." Invite everyone to contribute thoughts about these categories. They may include personal reasons, news-related issues, and concerns on behalf of others. Close in prayer with one person summarizing the list or by going around the circle and praying for each item listed.

99

HIGHS-AND-LOWS PRAYER ◄┄┄┄┄┄┄┐

Begin your time together by letting each person share a personal highlight and the low point of their week. Ask participants to reflect the joys and the concerns of each other in their prayers. Enhance the ritual of this share-prayer by creating a special name for it such as Lemons-Lemonade, Fright-Delight, Joys-Jabs, or www.prayer (for wow-worries-wonders).

100

SPONTANEOUS PRAYER

In day-to-day conversations or discussions with your family or youth group, critical issues or concerns often arise. Don't miss this prayer moment. Stop and pray for that issue before moving on.

101

FAITHTALK PRAYER ←┄┄┄┄┄┄┄┐

Susan's small group uses FaithTalk cards from The Youth & Family Institute. The cards invite people to share their memories and stories of faith. Each story becomes a prompt for prayer.

There are two sets of these cards: one for children and one for youth and older. Order them at www.youthandfamilyinstitute.org.

102

→ **JAVELIN PRAYER**

This prayer needs just a quick line, straight and to the point. These are prayers that can be prayed anytime, anywhere, either verbally or silently. For example:

- *God, give me guidance as I try to talk with Mom.*

- *Lord, forgive me for saying that to my friend.*

- *Help me understand.*

103

FOXHOLE PRAYER ◄┄┄┄┄┄┄┄┄┄┐

This is similar to the Javelin Prayer. During wartime battles soldiers look for their hastily dug holes—foxholes—to jump into for protection from attacks. This name, of course, comes from the animal, the fox, who retreats quickly into its den when sensing danger. Offering a quick prayer in time of trouble or panic is reminiscent of seeking the safety of a foxhole.

104

105

ARROW PRAYER

Often prayers are thought of as something that needs to be done at specific times and ways. This prayer format suggests a quick phrase that can be spoken or thought anytime and anywhere. Below are some examples of phrases based on scriptures. Invite participants to memorize and use short lines like short quick arrows carrying a message to God.

- I can do all things through him who strengthens me. *(Philippians 4:13: I can do all things through him who strengthens me.)*

- Help me to be quick to listen, slow to speak, and slow to become angry. *(James 1:19: You must understand this, my beloved: let everyone be quick to listen, slow to speak, slow to anger.)*

SITUATIONS

- Help me to put my hands to the plow and not look back. *(Luke 9:62: Jesus said to him, "No one who puts a hand to the plow and looks back is fit for the kingdom of God.")*

- Let me stand firm in all the will of God, mature and fully assured. *(Colossians 4:12: Epaphras, who is one of you, a servant of Christ Jesus, greets you. He is always wrestling in his prayers on your behalf, so that you may stand mature and fully assured in everything that God wills.)*

- Give me strength to guard my heart, for it is the wellspring of life. *(Proverbs 4:23: Keep your heart with all vigilance, for from it flow the springs of life.)*

- I will praise you, O Lord, with all my heart; I will tell of all your wonders. *(Psalm 9:1: I will give thanks to the Lord with my whole heart; I will tell of all your wonderful deeds.)*

PILLOW PRAYER

Place a small stone (bigger is not better in this case) on your pillow when you make your bed each morning. When you go to bed at night, the prayer rock awaits you as a reminder of God's constant care and a time to pray.

106

ALL-THRU-THE-NIGHT PRAYER EVENT

Kristin's congregation joins others in the county for an all-night prayer fest. They use a number of forms of prayer. The experience is multi-sensory, with PowerPoint® visuals and music/worship provided by the local college praise band.

107

PARTNER PRAYER

108

Relationships are strengthened through prayer. For some, praying in pairs can be less intimidating then praying in groups. Assign prayer partners for a session, a month, or a whole year at time. Prayer partners may choose to make a commitment to call or e-mail each other during the week to mutually learn what's happening in each other's life, or they may decide to meet. Invite pairs to sit together and summarize what each has heard from his or her partner in the form of a prayer.

NAME PRAYER ◄┄┄┄┄┐

Names are powerful reminders of who we are. They were given to us at birth and spoken aloud at baptism and other milestones in our lives. Pray a thanksgiving prayer for your own gifts, abilities, traits, and joys, choosing words that begin with each letter of your name. (Lyle's been pondering what the Y in his name represents. Don't worry, Lyle—we'll just start calling you ol' yeller!)

109

COUNTDOWN PRAYER

We were saying blessing prayers for a friend who was off to interview for a new job. One person prayed and then started to count down. *10, 9, 8, 7, 6....* The countdown got quieter with each number. Before we got very far, another person began to pray. After she finished, the countdown started again. This happened about eight different times until we finally reached 0. The prayer time was over and we all said, "Amen."

110

A.B.C. PRAYER

It's back to Sesame Street! "Today's prayer is brought to you by the letters J and C."

Going around the circle, each person prays for one thing he or she is thankful for. The first person prays for something that begins with the letter A; the second person, B; the third, C—you get the idea. It works well and can be quite sincere except for those honestly trying to be thankful for xylophones and zebras!

111

THAT-REMINDS-ME PRAYER

112

As one prays for safety in travels, another remembers a neighbor who is flying to see a heart specialist, which reminds someone else of a friend who is in a hospital, which in turn reminds another of an aunt who just got out of the hospital after giving birth. In conversation, one person's spoken words often lead to the next person's thoughts. It can be the same with prayer. Participants take turns praying. Each person listens carefully to the previous person's prayer, then begins with the words, "Lord, that reminds me...."

ROBERT'S-RULES-OF-ORDER PRAYER FORMAT

This is a simplified version of the Peer Prayer.

1. **Name it.** Make a prayer list.

2. **Propose it.** Seek volunteers to pray for it.

3. **Second it.** Make a commitment to pray.

4. **Adopt it.** Pray through the week.

5. **Check it.** Answered? Completed? Continue?

113

PEER PRAYER

This pattern of prayer may appear complicated. It combines several of the prayer forms listed previously and is a powerful source of encouragement as peers or family members commit to praying for one another. Use it at the close of a youth group gathering, Sunday school, campfire, or family devotions. It is done in five stages:

1. **Name it.** Each person identifies a situation or person to be prayed for. *(Teresa says, "My mother's having surgery tomorrow.")*

2. **Adopt it.** Each person agrees to pray for another's concern. *(Nick says, "I'd like to pray for Teresa's mom.")*

114

3. **Commit to it.** Each person restates the situation and explains what they will pray for. *(Nick says, "Teresa and her family are very worried about her mom's upcoming surgery. I'll pray for the family as they face this challenge.")*

4. **Pray it.** Throughout the week, continue to pray for that particular concern.

5. **Revisit it.** Take time to ask about your special prayer concern. *(Nick asks, "Teresa, how is your mom? How is the rest of the family doing?")*

Begin the whole process again.

SECRET PRAYER PARTNERS

Each participant is given the name of another participant, and is to keep the name a secret over a designated number of days, weeks, or months—whatever works best for your group. During that period of time, each person observes her or his secret partner with special attention to concerns, gifts, needs, and cause for thanksgiving, and then regularly prays for the partner. An occasional note of encouragement or support might also be shared. At the end of the designated time period, hold a "revelation party" where the partners reveal themselves to each other.

115

OREO® PRAYER ←┄┄┄┄┄┄┄┄┐

The filling in the middle does the praying! Stand or sit in a
circle while joining hands. Ask each participant to silently say
a prayer for the person to his or her right, and then for the
person to the left, and then for themselves. Everyone will
know that three prayers have been shared on their behalf.
Serve Oreo® or other sandwich cookies afterward.

116

SANDWICH PRAYER

Here's a variation on the Oreo® Prayer. Form the group into triads. Ask each group of three to find a space away from the others. Follow the Oreo® Prayer experience, but this time pray out loud instead of silently.

117

QUEEN/KING-FOR-A-DAY PRAYER

Each time your group or family meets, select one person to be the subject of prayer for that time or day. That person gets to be the queen or king for the day, meaning she or he will get the respect and attention that royalty would get every day. This allows individuals to take turns having the focus and honor of others' prayers.

118

PICK-A-WORD PRAYER

Need some words to get started? Encourage your participants to come up with a list of attributes, a list of images and a list of feelings. Picking a word from each list is often enough for a person who is not used to praying aloud get a good start. Encourage participants to continue the prayer by describing the reason for their feeling. The release of feeling can be an incredible experience of honesty with God.

CINQUIN PRAYER

This simple form of five-line poetry is easily applied to prayers to be shared with the wider community. The pattern is as follows.

Line 1—a one-word title

Line 2—two words to describe the title

Line 3—three words of action relating to title

Line 4—four words of feeling relating to title

Line 5—one word that refers back to title

Example: *Mercy*
Undeserved compassion
God's unconditional love
When I feel ashamed
Forgiven

120

MARKED WITH THE CROSS OF CHRIST

Invite each participant to develop a signature that incorporates a discreet cross or other faith symbol in or beside the letters. Whenever the person uses the signature, the incorporated symbol can serve as a quick reminder to offer a short prayer—a prayer related to that particular situation or person involved with the reason for signing his or her name. It will also affirm not only *who* you are but *whose* you are.

121

JOURNAL PRAYER

122

Those who keep prayer journals often express how awesome it is to look back and track the various ways God hears and responds. Groups or families can keep a prayer journal together. Include the date, the joy or concern, and the name of the person seeking prayer. Each time you meet, look back over the requests. Add notes as to how the requests were answered. What a great way to help participants continue to pray for joys and concerns and to say, "Thank you, God."

"DEAR GOD" PRAYER ←·······

123

"Dear God, it's me."

Writing a letter is one of the most intimate forms of communication. When people are serious about relationships, they put it in writing. Keep a diary of letters to God as an occasional reminder of the various ways our God in heaven hears and answers.

CROSSWORD PRAYER

Use a sheet of grid paper. Pick prayer topics that can be represented with one-word answers. One person begins by writing a word such as *hunger, grandma,* or *healing* in the middle of the paper, putting one letter in each square.

124

The person says a verbal prayer for the topic. Subsequent prayer petitions are offered in the same manner, written in squares, either up or down, sharing at least one letter with another word in the same way a crossword puzzle would look.

```
        P E A C E
              O
            A U N T
              N
              T
H U N G E R
              Y
```

BASKETFUL OF PRAYERS ←·······┐

Many churches invite worshipers to write prayer requests and to leave them in the offering plate. Then, the prayer team gathers weekly to pray over these requests. Groups or families can do the same thing. Each person writes a prayer request on an index card and places it in a basket. The cards can either be signed or left anonymous. Ask everyone to pull a card from the basket, exchanging it if it is his or her own. Take turns praying for the requests.

125

VESSEL FOR PRAYERS

Here's a variation on Basket Full of Prayers and an occasion to start your own tradition. Do you have a vessel for the prayer requests? How about that sombrero from your Mexican mission trip, a plastic jack-o-lantern left over from the Halloween party, the pastor's favorite ball cap, a ceramic candy dish, or anything else that holds special meaning for your group or family?

126

WINK PRAYER ←

Sitting in a restaurant, 63-year-old Bob asks others at the table whether he could offer his restaurant prayer. He removes his glasses, looks up, and winks! What a great way of acknowledging the presence of God, particularly in the midst of life's stresses and celebrations.

"Excuse me is there something in your eye?"

"No, just praying!"

127

BLOWN KISS PRAYER

Kevin shares this simple act of devotion from a friend who is a nun. Before she eats a meal she puts the ends of her fingers together on one hand, lightly kisses the fingertips, and then raises her hand, blowing her kiss upward.

128

THUMBS-UP PRAYER

Use a mealtime prayer to simply say, "Hey, God, thanks," as you give an exuberant thumbs-up sign.

129

SIGN OF THE CROSS IN MY WHOLE BEING

Do this individually or in pairs, each person making the sign of the cross over the other. Make the sign of the cross over:

• Ears—for listening to God's voice and hearing God's word

• Eyes—for seeing God's glory in all life

• Lips—for boldly speaking the name of Christ and speaking of God's power to others

• Heart—for remembering that we are God's own, named and claimed and showered with love

• Shoulders—for willingness to serve as Jesus served and bear the yoke of others

• Hands—for work and service that Christ will be known

• Feet—for following Christ and walking in his steps

HEART IGNITE: ENGAGING PRAYER EXPERIENCES

130

BODY PRAYER ◄┄┄┄┄┄┄

After you use this prayer, you'll wonder whether a person is scratching their head or praying really hard! Listeners touch their body parts and listed below and pray silently, hearing the prompt that follows:

131

- Top of the head—*Remember the ways you experience God's loving presence in your life.*
- Forehead—*Ask for God's guidance and wisdom.*
- Mouth—*Speak kindly and with Christ's love.*
- Ears—*Listen to others and seek to understand.*
- Heart—*Ask for compassion and a sense of others' needs.*
- Belly—*Feel deeply, remembering joy…and sorrow.*
- Hand—*You serve as Jesus served others.*
- Knees—*We humble ourselves to the Lord of our life!*
- Legs—*We walk in the way of the Lord.*

HEART IGNITE: ENGAGING PRAYER EXPERIENCES

MOTION PRAYER

A series of motions speak a silent prayer:

1. Position yourself in an attitude of prayer with hands folded in front of the body.

2. Slowly raise hands, still folded, above the head with arms outstretched, seeking God's presence.

3. Gradually open hands and arms, fully prepared to receive whatever God has to offer.

4. Slowly and intentionally, bring arms down to the chest, crossing one over the other, bringing gifts from God to your heart. Hold them and cherish them. Give thanks.

5. Open arms out toward others. Touch those next to you, symbolically giving your God-given gifts away. Share with others the love God gave you.

132

BEFORE-OR-AFTER-A-MEAL ◄┄┄┄┄┄┄┐
PRAYER

Use the following gestures to give thanks to our God, the provider.

133

• Point upward—a gesture inviting God's presence.

• Touch two fingers to the lips—an action for eating.

• Pat the stomach—the fulfilled nourishment of food.

• Form a fist with a thumb pointing upward—giving the thumbs-up sign to say thank you.

SIGN-OF-THE-CROSS PRAYER

"As a family we always end the day with a prayer followed by tracing the cross on each other's forehead. It is a family ritual that reminds us every day who we are and to whom we belong."

Such traditions can enrich any family or small-group experience. Start a similar one in your group.

134

CLENCHED FIST PRAYER ◄

Ask participants to close their eyes, form a fist, and hold it out in front of themselves, keeping the fingers down and the back of the fist up. Let this clenched fist represent the hurts, pains, and mistakes of life. Ask participants to recall a time when somebody hurt them and they have not been able to forgive. Encourage them to remember the impure thoughts, the occasions when mistakes hurt another, when someone was ignored, or even when God was pushed aside. Imagine the hurts and brokenness being held in the tightly clenched fists. Slowly read Romans 8:38-39: "For I am convinced that neither death, nor life, nor angels, nor rulers, nor things present, nor things to come, nor powers, nor height, nor depth, nor anything else in all creation, will be able to separate us from the love of God in Christ Jesus our Lord." During the scripture reading, people may open their fist, turn their palms upward, and open their eyes.

135

HEART IGNITE: ENGAGING PRAYER EXPERIENCES

NAIL PRAYER

"The large cross and the very personal prayers hanging there for all to read touched me. I guess that's what happens on a cross; nothing is hidden, everyone can look on."

Write prayers on slips of paper and use small nails to nail them to a large wooden cross. Participants can choose to sign the prayers or leave them anonymous. If you are working with a group that lacks skills in Hammering 101, a cross drawn on chart paper and sticky notes could be the answer for you.

136

"ONE ANOTHERING" PRAYER

Begin and end this prayer experience with these words:

I seek to listen more closely to others' needs. I seek to pray for someone other than myself. I know the peace and comfort of having someone else hear me and pray on my behalf. In Jesus' name we pray.

Each person shares a personal prayer concern. As individual requests are made, others listen intently and each person agrees to pray for another. One by one, hear the prayers aloud. Conclude by again praying the phrases above.

137

HEALING-AND-BLESSING PRAYER

Often an individual will share deeply from the heart about special needs, decisions looming, or sensitive issues. Invite the person to kneel while others lay a hand on her or his head or shoulder, offering prayers for healing or blessing.

138

BANDAGE PRAYER ◄┄┄┄┄┄┄┄┐

Ouch! When a heartfelt concern is expressed about a person who is hurting from physical, social, spiritual, or mental pains, say a prayer. Ask God to give peace and strength in the midst of pain and healing. Put a bandage on the back of the person's hand as a reminder of the prayers shared. ┄┄┘

139

→ STONE NOT THROWN

140

I keep a river stone in my desk with John 8:7 ("Let anyone among you who is without sin be the first to throw a stone...") written on it. The verse comes from the story about the women caught in adultery, and is a poignant and vivid reminder that I must not judge others. Our youth group was going through some difficult times with gossip, exclusion, and triangulation. I painted John 8:7 on a bucketful of stones. At the closing prayer time, I read the passage and invited each person to reflect on relationships within the group. "What stones do you hold in your hand? Jealousy, anger, resentment? Who are you aiming them at?" We closed with prayer. Some prayed silently. Others felt moved to name the illness plaguing our group, confessing and seeking forgiveness. With the final amen everyone was asked to leave in silence and to pick up a stone to take home—the stone not thrown.

HEART IGNITE: ENGAGING PRAYER EXPERIENCES

WASHED AWAY PRAYER ◄┈┈┈┈┈┈┈┈┐

This is a powerful symbolic experience of God's forgiveness. With a washable marker, each person writes on his or her palm one sin they want washed away. Place a basin of water, soap, and a towel in the center of the group. People take turns washing their hands while offering a silent prayer. Conclude with an affirmation such as, "Through the waters of baptism and God's everlasting grace, know that your sins are forgiven." The amen comes as everyone raises their clean palms!

141

CALENDAR PRAYER

Someone shares that next Thursday it will be two years since Grandpa died, another shares that her trip to the mountains is coming up, while another shares the date his Mom is scheduled for surgery.

Lay out a large copy of the present month's calendar where everyone can see it. Invite each person to lay a small object such as a ring, pen cap, coin, or other marker on the date that holds particular significance. Let each person identify the marker and share the reason for the date chosen. As each prayer-story is told, the speaker ends by saying, "Lord in your mercy," and others respond, "Hear our prayer."

142

TAKE-HOME CALENDAR ◄┈┈┈┈┈┈┈┐

This calendar prayer also invites people to share high-
lights and concerns for the month to come. A workshop
participant told how he invites people to write short
notes followed by their name on a blank calendar page.
He then photocopies the page and gives each participant
a copy to take home and post in a place that will remind
them to pray daily throughout the month.

143

SEVEN-DAYS-A-WEEK PRAYER

Those in your family or group who thrive on patterns and ritual will especially appreciate this prayer. This weekly prayer guide will provide a "trellis" on which to hang prayers. Invite the group to shape the topics according to your context or situation. Here's one example:

Sunday—relationship with God
 (faithfulness, revelation, holiness)

Monday—relationship with family
 (immediate and extended)

Tuesday—relationship with others
 (friends, teachers, acquaintances)

144

Wednesday—spiritual guidance
   (pure motives, enlightenment, mission mindedness)

Thursday—protection
   (temptation, deception, physical harm)

Friday—body, head, heart, and spirit
   (mental, physical, and spiritual wholeness)

Saturday—priorities and blessings
   (put first things first, give thanks)

AFFIRMATION JAR PRAYER

145

This may be used over a period of time, such as a series of meetings, a month of home devotions, a retreat, or a stay at camp. Each person has his or her own jar (or sand pail, decorated coffee can, or other object that will hold a collection of paper slips). Others write prayers of encouragement and thanksgiving for that person and place them in the owner's jar. At the end of the time period, open the jars and have an affirmation ceremony. Pray together a prayer that affirms relationships with one another and with God.

AFFIRMATION-AND-BLESSING PRAYER

Use the following blessing prayer for each person.

I see (name a gift, character trait, act of kindness) *in you*

when you (give a specific example),

which makes me (feel, want to, wish, or hope).

May God bless you with (understanding, hope, guidance, power, etc.)

Example: *Dear Lord, I see in Monique the ability to hear and understand others. She has demonstrated this as she listened to me talk about my dad. I feel comfort as I felt understood. Bless her as she plants seeds and nurtures their growth, helping people to know your love, grace, power, and forgiveness.*

146

GRAFFITI HEART PRAYER

At the church or at home, post a large piece of chart paper or poster board. Title it with "What's on your heart?" and draw several hearts in various shapes and sizes. Over time, encourage the youth or family to regularly stop at the graffiti sheet to write a prayer concern in one of the hearts. Gather at the end of youth meetings or every few days with the family to talk about the heartfelt concerns and/or joys and to pray over them.

147

TISSUE SQUARES PRAYER

Pass around a roll of toilet tissue. Ask each person to take as many squares as they think they will need for their prayer. Now, for each square they are to pray one petition.

148

ACCORDION FOLD PRAYER

Fold a blank sheet of paper into an accordion. Make each fold about about ¾" deep. Unfold the paper. As you pray this prayer, the group will fold the sheet back into the accordion shape.

Choose a prayer topic such as "things I'm thankful for," "my biggest concern today," or "people to pray for." The first person writes her or his thought along the bottom of the paper, below the crease, then creates the first accordion fold, covering what was just written. The second person writes on the fold and then covers the writing. This continues until everyone has written on a fold. One person opens and reads each petition, followed by "Lord, in your mercy," and the response, "Hear our prayer."

149

IN-YOUR-MITT PRAYER ←············

Ask each person to write the name of someone he or she is concerned about on a piece of paper. Fold the papers so the names don't show, stack them, and clip them together. Pass the stack of papers around the circle. Each person folds his or her hands around the stack of papers and offers a silent or spoken prayer. This visible reminder of the power of the gathered community illumines our need to call upon one another to pray unceasingly.

150

PAPER TOWEL PRAYER

This can be a bit complicated but is a wonderful way to invite your group or family to pray for one another every day. It is best to do this one month at time. Each person needs a roll of white paper towels. Ultimately one prayer concern will be written with markers on each sheet of toweling. (Sheets should not be separated.) The subject of the prayers will come as you ask individuals in the group to name concerns in their own lives or in the congregation, community, or world. Very carefully, reroll the paper towels. At home, every day, tear off one sheet and lift up prayers for that particular person or concern.

151

PAPER AIRPLANE PRAYER

Ask each person to write a simple prayer request or a list of prayer concerns on a sheet of paper. Form it into a paper airplane and shoot it across the circle of participants, each person catching someone else's plane. When everyone has a plane in hand, go around the circle and have each person offer the prayer on behalf of another.

152

COOTIE CATCHER PRAYER

Not familiar with a cootie catcher? Ask any elementary school child how to make this simple, folded paper toy and how to use it! Inside each fold of paper have the child, youth, or, yes, even adult, write a specific topic of prayer such as hunger, friends, and family. Call out, "Pray!" to get the game started. At each stopping point in the game, a flap of paper is unfolded to reveal a topic of prayer. Pause for a moment to pray about the topic revealed, and then continue the game.

153

TP=TOTALLY PRAYED

Kristine and her youth group give new meaning to the time-honored tradition of "TP-ing" someone's house. They form small groups and visit the homes of other youth in the congregation or anyone needing a little attention. They offer a prayer for the family, and then they leave a square of toilet paper with the words "You have been TPed—totally prayed for—by the youth of _____," and each person signs the square!

154

SCHOOL BUS PRAYER

Each morning when Jane and her car-pool buddies sees that familiar yellow school bus, they speak a brief prayer that the bus driver and students travel in safety and that their day be blessed.

155

RAILROAD TRACK PRAYER

Here's a time-honored tradition in many families and youth groups traveling in a car or bus. Each time you cross railroad tracks, everyone (except the driver!) raises their feet and offers prayers for a safe journey.

HEART IGNITE: ENGAGING PRAYER EXPERIENCES

SIREN PRAYER

The shrill alarm of a siren signals the presence of pain, sickness, fear, fire, violence, or compromised safety. Let the sound of an ambulance, fire truck, or police car be occasion for spontaneous prayers of healing, comfort, wisdom, and safety for all involved.

157

SAFE JOURNEY PRAYER ←┈┈┈┈┈┈┐

Before taking a trip across town or across the state, use the vehicle to remind you of prayers needed. Point to...

- The vehicle—that those inside use the journey to build caring relationships, and treat others in Christ-like ways

- Wheels—that all who share the road are alert, patient, and driving with caution

- Steering wheel—that God guides the travelers to their destination; that their purpose there be meaningful and brings glory to God

- Seat belt—that all are kept secure in God's caring arms

- Gas peddle and brakes—that the driver be given wisdom, attentiveness, patience, and energy

- Horn—for sharing the joy found in Christ Jesus!

158

ROAD RAGE PRAYER

Eunice has the perfect way of dealing with other drivers who aren't paying attention, nearly run others off the road, pretend not to see signals, tailgate, or are totally engaged in their cell-phone conversations. In these cases, Eunice sees two options. One involves an expression of anger; the other, Eunice suggests, is to pray for the safety of that driver and all vehicles he or she encounters.

159

PRAYER PROMISES ◄ ┄┄┄┄┄┄┄┄┄┄┄

The following scriptures assure us of God's promises and faithfulness in hearing and responding to our prayers. Read these promises at the end of a prayer time or between various petitions as individuals share their prayers.

- Matthew 6:6 ("...your Father who sees in secret will reward you.")

- Matthew 7:7-8 ("Knock and the door will be opened....")

- John 14:13-14 ("I will do whatever you ask in my name....)

- John 15:7 ("If you abide in me....")

- John 15:16 ("...the Father will give you whatever you ask....")

- John 16:24 ("...so that your joy may be complete.")

160

PERSONALIZED SCRIPTURE PRAYER

161

Many of the psalms and other scriptures can be personalized by inserting a person's name. Psalm 91 is an example. Mary, who dwells in the shelter of the Most High, will rest in the shadow of the Almighty. Larry will say to the Lord, "His is my refuge and my fortress, my God, in whom I trust. He will cover Terry with his feathers, and under his wings Barry will find refuge."

BIBLE PRAYERS ◄┄┄┄┄┄┐

Pray the prayers found in Scripture. Here's a starter list. Read, listen, reflect, and pray.

- Song of Moses (Exodus 15:1-8)

- Song of Deborah (Judges 5:2-31)

- Solomon's prayer (I Kings 3:6-9)

- Hannah's prayer (1 Samuel 2:1-10)

- David's prayer (Psalm 51)

- Magnificat (Luke 1:46-55)

- Benedictus (Luke 1:68-79)

- Lord's Prayer (Matthew 6:9-13)

- Stephen's prayer (Acts 7:60)

- Tax collector's prayer (Luke 18:13)

- Christ's prayer for all believers (John 17)

- Paul's prayer (Ephesians 3:14-21)

162

TIPPY CANOE PRAYER

When devotions are held at a river, stream, or lake, ask each person to select a piece of fallen bark, twig, leaf, or pinecone resembling a small boat or canoe. As prayers are spoken, each person places their boat-prayer into the water, to be carried away by the current, symbolically in God's care.

163

PSALMS-ACROSS-THE-WATER PRAYER

For a memorable experience, form participants into two groups separated by a stream, a small lake, or other natural setting. Read and pray a psalm antiphonally to one another. Praise psalms such as Psalms 136, 138, 145, 146, and 148 may be appropriate.

164

PICK-A-CARD-ANY-CARD PRAYER

Megan, Drew, and Kendra recall that when they were small, they wrote their favorite Sunday school and VBS songs on small pieces of poster board. At mealtime, each person took a turn selecting a card and leading the musical blessing!

165

BOUQUET OF BLESSINGS ◄┄┄┄┄┄┄┐

Brenda was invited to dinner. In the center of the table was an arrangement of "homegrown" construction-paper flowers. Attached to each flower was a tag with a different mealtime prayer. When it came time to pray, the young daughter was invited to pick a flower from the arrangement. and read the prayer.

Invite your group or family to share favorite mealtime prayers. Type the prayers, photocopy them, and put them on small cards and then create your own bouquets.

166

PRAYER LOG

....

Keep track of the prayers you have used
and how you used them.

Prayer Number	Date Used	Event or Occasion	Comments and Ideas

Prayer Number	Date Used	Event or Occasion	Comments and Ideas

PRAYER THOUGHTS

....

Pray *about* something, not *for* something!

To be a Christian without prayer is no more possible than to be alive without breathing. —*Martin Luther*

If I should neglect prayer but a single day, I should lose a great deal of the fire of faith. —*Martin Luther*

We may pray most when we say least, and we may pray least when we say most. —*St. Augustine of Hippo*

Prayer is not conquering God's reluctance, but taking hold of God's willingness. —*Phillips Brooks*

The best prayers often have more groans than words. —*John Bunyan*

Countless people pray far more than they know. Often they have such a "stained-glass" image of prayer that they fail to recognize what they are experiencing as prayer and so condemn themselves for not praying. —*Richard J. Foster*

Remember that you can pray any time, anywhere. Washing dishes, digging ditches, working in the office, in the shop, on the athletic field, even in prison—you can pray and know God hears! —*Billy Graham*

Prayer is nothing else than a sense of God's presence.
—*Brother Lawrence*

Do not make prayer a monologue—make it a conversation.
—*Unknown*

Don't tell God how big your problems are, tell your problems how BIG GOD is! —*Unknown*

CONTINUED

Prayer begins with silence to allow the Holy Spirit to shape and form our words. —*Unknown*

DID YOU KNOW...

The word *bead* comes from the Old English word *gebed* meaning "prayer" and the Middle English word *bede,* "to pray." Hey, get out those beads!

Lectio Divina is an ancient practice of sacred reading as a way of prayer. *Lectio*=reading; *divina*=sacred.